Praise for *When the World Ends This Time*

"Much like the new home the speaker is building for herself, so does this chapbook take you into her little world of nostalgia, tenderness, longing, acceptance, renewal, and growth. This is a timely, thought-provoking read during what truly does feel like the end of the world, but that leaves you with a sense of wistfulness and cautious hopefulness." — Sofia Aguilar, author of *amor*

"Paula Macena's latest collection, *When the World Ends This Time*, is concise and cutthroat. Macena makes poetry out of the details in the stories she shares, navigating this life. These poems are confessions and invite introspection for anyone who feels like the world is ending." — Zane Frederick, author of *i am tired of being a dandelion*

"Macena has written an honestly raw collection of poems. They take you on a beautifully written journey of self-discovery and healing. It's an absolute treat." - Raquel Franco, author of *I'll Cry If I Want To*

"*When the World Ends This Time* is a poignant and honest exploration into the often murky waters of identity, love and place (and where they intermingle). A visceral search for home, for meaning, and triumphantly—a dance with the unanswered questions that many of us are too afraid to ask." - Sonja Ringo, author of *Where the Beetle Went for Lunch*

To my many homes away from home

When the World Ends This Time

Paula Macena

Contents

"I'll

Give I'll

Give I'll

Give I'll

Give I'll

Give you all

I can give I'll

Give I'll

Give I'll

Give you everything that I'll

Give I'll

Give I'll

Give I'll

Give I'll

Give you all I can

Give I'll

Give I'll

Give I'll

Give"

— Dogs on Shady Lane, *Cole St*

In A World Where Everything Goes Right,

I am cotton candy sweet
(the melt-on-your-tongue type that
my mother always wanted from me). I grew up
mean,   my knees a little too
            scraped and my tongue

a little too sharp. When we kissed,
I didn't know what to make
of all your kindness
(looking up at you,   the way you never
wished I would).   I'm sorry,

I can't live in the delusion that I could
ever be your equal. (I've been hoarding you till
Christmas, till New Year's, but my jaw
aches and my   hands are full,)
            Baby, I'm selfish.

I don't think I can learn to get
enough of anything. You give with your
palms wide open while my
fists   are clenched.
Unravel   them gently.

Teach me, I ask. I've never

considered myself kind (but you've

considered me kinder). My cheeks

aren't fully   rounded out yet—

        I know that now. You showed me that.

Under the Bed

Floorboards, and beneath that:

1. A chasm you attempted to fill with CDs.
2. A treasure chest of leftovers.
3. A hovel of attempts.
4. You know there's a Bible in here, somewhere (you lost it in the mess).
5. You lost all your hair ties, too.
6. A piece of gum stuck beneath the right side of your bed (put your hand in the right place, fingerprint on fingerprint, it becomes part of you again, you are her   again).

Your best friend's mother

cooks spaghetti in an apartment
that reeks of childhood.
You are eight and you
haven't yet figured out how to swim.
Your best friend's mother
tells you that the trick is buoyancy
but you're not so sure. You think it lies
somewhere between
the small of your back and the water,
the gap, you tell her, between skin and
surface tension.
She laughs, asks you if you believe
Jesus walked on water or if
the curves of his feet rested
on that gap. You shrug.
You don't tell her that God
didn't give you all the answers
yet; he shoved them all in that
little gap, and is waiting for you to learn.

A Lesson on Point of View

My story is told by an outside narration;
    [meaning, that my third-person perspective

    makes my entire life an out-of-body experience;]

    [meaning, that I am the author

    and the protagonist both.]

So when I say I am the product of my own downfall,
    [I mean that I still remember

    being small and skinny and seventeen.]

    [I mean I remember turning the ends

    of my veins into grenades;

    my wrists into florets of self-hatred,]

    [I mean to fit the smallest of my doubts

    without them oozing out of my skin.]

    [Meaning that being nineteen and

    picking at the cracks

    to get out the last of my epiphanies

    isn't very fun.]

Maybe my healing became my addiction
and now that's why my hands
always fail to feel like my hands.

Freeze-Frame Absent of Cavities

In 2016, we found out
>   the world had moved on without us
>   and we couldn't remember a thing about it.

I'm busy dyeing your hair in my bathroom,
>   the sink blood's reflection, your
>   dead ends like yarn in my hands—

You left your toothbrush at home, you say,
>   I let you use mine while your hair turns red,
>   we wait for the timer to count down to midnight

and the world spins on its axis. It's still
>   2016, you think, there's still time to rinse
>   this down the drain, a whirlpool of your

dead ends, your name—there's time, you
>   think. So you spit in the sink. You
>   wash your hair. The timer never
>   goes off.

It Goes Like This:

You're singing
that song again.
The one you
know but forgot.
The one that
everybody knows
and nobody loves.
And you think
there's a metaphor,
somewhere in
there, because
you always think
that you're some-
thing greater (or
much much worse)
than you really are.

You know that there
are lots of reasons for
you being the way you
are. You know that none
of them matter. You
keep singing that song.
That stupid song that
everybody knows and
you've never loved. You
stare at yourself in the
mirror and hum the same
tune and try to be human
and you know it goes
something like this but
you always choke, why
do you always choke?

You convince yourself that you are fine because you are.
You convince yourself that you are fine because you are.
You convince yourself that you are fine because you are.
You convince yourself that you are fine.

A Thing That Tries

We keep clinging to necks
that aren't ours. / I am baring my
teeth at your hips / and picturing
you at the lake, the snow, / this thing
shining blue and wet and / hoping
for a future nearly as bright. / Your
love is a thing that tries. / It's a thing
that gets up / when it shouldn't. It's
like when / a good thing doesn't
know when to die, / when a live
thing has / curled into itself.
Eyelashes sipping / frost in the air,
fingertips red and raw / with truth,
with cold. Reaching / with palms up.
Asking for tomorrow.

Me Fala Com Sua Alma

My novelty wore off,
and I've never known my first language to be anything
but an accent that I couldn't wrap my tongue around.
Parece forçado, you say,

                  and all I can do is laugh.

There's nothing I don't have a complicated relationship with;
and I could weave this tapestry all I want,
it won't make this home country a home.
Dizendo que sou americana

                  não vai me tornar americana.

For the past year, I have been playing hide and seek with
myself—
I'm a lost and found of cities I've never lingered in long
enough,
hallmarks that stretch for miles but remain out of sight—
my greatest fantasy

                  is to settle.

To feel satisfied without this rat race breathing
down my neck. Me fala com sua alma.
Tell me what you really want:

a bed that feels

                  like a second skin

and a room warm enough to stay.

Give me shelter but don't hold me hostage;

leave the door open on your way out.

Espero que você tropece ao sair,

                  mas nunca hesite em voltar.

Suburban

Legacies never

last long when they're

founded on a cul-de-sac.

Around the corner

from Van Buren Ave,

there's a steep driveway lined

with perennial clovers.

You pick them—

Commit their shape

to memory.

When the apocalypse comes,

you like to think

this will be the first to go.

Stroudsburg, Pennsylvania

Anyway, my hair has grown out now and the tea is getting cold / and I still remember how the stairs creaked in your old house, / how you'd sit on the landing with your head in your hands. / You taught me that there are things that are not supposed to work out; / you taught me how to want those things anyway. / But much to our dismay, sometimes the only thing left to do / is what we're told. Is to close the blinds and / sleep early after all. I've memorized how your / weight feels on my chest and those rickety stairs, / I remember everything but the sound of your voice. / Take all of this with a grain of salt, and by that I mean / just take it. We're just blowing cold air / anyway. The point is, there are things that are not supposed to work out but / you want it to, you want it to and / will you let me make my own mistakes? / Anyway, I'll cut my hair next week and put the kettle back on the stove, / and you'll go back up the stairs and skip the creaking step / and you won't have aged a day.

Exodus 33, Moses Sees God's Back

I didn't know that I could have
       conversations about God until
       I was twenty-two.

a. When a moth is drawn to a flame,
      in the seconds before it dies,
      it witnesses what we will
      never comprehend.

b. Moses asked to see God. He stood
      in the crevice of a mountain and
      watched God pass him by,
      a flicker in the gap
      between our universe and his.

c. How similar are we to moths
      that we risk our lives just to
      get a glimpse of
      something beautiful?

Hometown Prophet

I am constantly convinced I'm the most unlikable person
        ever, but I'll blame it on being from New Jersey.
My guiltiest pleasure is eating on a train with dirty subway
        hands, speaking a foreign language in native streets,

but when you leave home, when does it stop being home?
        When your shelter was nothing but a bomb, do you
army crawl your way out, belly full of dirt, or
        do you find comfort in the rubble?

When you visit home, tell me: do you feel like a guest
        or a god? Tell me the best myths you've heard about
yourself; tell me how many are true. Do you
        know if their hands ever stop reaching?

Everywhere is the smallest fucking town I've ever lived
        and there is nowhere that I won't find you. There's
something to say for this, and by that I mean there's nothing
        to show. You are my only evidence of a life well-lived.

Look at the palm trees and remember why you came here.
Remember why it mattered. Your hands are still dirty,
greedy, but just because you're afraid of holding on doesn't
mean you were supposed to let go. Doesn't mean
you ever did.

Bruegel

We'll start with the flowers:

>both the dead and alive, both sitting

>on your kitchen counter

>and out in the yard.

>I think there are things we're not

>supposed to know

>so we can enjoy things like this:

>wisterias, hanging limply,

>and a fox crossing through your yard.

>The birds speak in languages we can't understand

>because we'd tear them apart if we did.

>We thought the tower of Babel was destroyed,

>but there it stands, tall in our backyards.

>I think there are things we're not supposed to know

>so we don't dissect them to death.

I am waiting to love myself again.
My teeth are crooked and their gaps fail to hold
any whispers of anything that matters.
I remember the room with the stained mattresses, their
springs digging into my ribs.

I remember the vines climbing the walls,
how I wished my roots would grow. Instead: there's a
welcome mat trampled by the door, and
I don't have it in me to straighten it out anymore.

I am waiting to love myself again
and to stop trying to make everything beautiful.
But there's a sweet melancholy in your empty
coatrack, and you text me when you need me,

and I think there's a poem in there, somewhere.
I can't keep trying to make this beautiful,
yet I know I will continue to drink from your cup
long after you are gone.

I am waiting to love myself again.
My fake tooth is begging for a second chance,
she says, "I want to be whole again." I'm sorry—

I'm still trying to get over the sound of my own voice.

I am waiting to love myself again.
Your affection is counterproductive, and my eyelashes keep
getting caught in yours. I can't tell where I begin and
you end, but god,

I can't keep trying to be you anymore.

I am waiting to love myself again
and I hope that I shave my eyebrows one day. My head,
too. I hope I'm not afraid of its shape.

I hope I won't lose weight to do it,
because that's what you would ask me to do—
and I can't be her for you anymore.

I am waiting to love myself again
and I think I might forgive you when I hold the
razor in my hand. When I shed the last of your skin.

I hope my tooth remains in half,
and my identity intact. This is no longer
beautiful, but I think you knew that by now.

Pass me a knife.
The tomato is set
on the cutting board,
and your hands are already
sticky with the juice.
Come, let's talk over wine
about how the girl next door
doesn't know how to mince
her garlic.
If she hears us,
we'll invite her over
and hold her hands
and guide her to a meal
she could never make alone.

Ode to Golden Girl
after Frank Ocean

There's a type of poetry held in oranges
        that I know I'll never be able to hold within myself.

How foolish of me, how childlike,
        to envy a fruit named after a color brighter

than any future I could ever imagine.
        We split heaven by its corners

and are kind enough to share it in halves,
        quarters, anything close enough

to resemble an offering from your childhood church.
        You know that they break bread at communion,

but here, in bed, you peel this orange back in fractions—
        telling yourself, your lover, that it's holier

than anything they could ever offer,
        than anything they've ever seen.

When the world ends this time,

you know what to do.
You hoard the worst of your abilities and store them
where the sun don't shine; you try not to feel aghast
at the possibilities, try not to think that something
must've flipped upside down along the way.

When the world ends this time, your mom tells you
nothing will happen. Calls you a doomsdayer,
your dad tells you to love people anyway,
but the dead know nothing, speak nothing—
so if your murderer spits on your grave, where will
the love go now?

When the world ends this time, your friend asks you
to come over. She is a plane ride away and you crave
the comfort of her couch, the smell of smoke in her
car. You want to watch her kiss on the dance floor
in the only act of rebellion you know you have,
that you are clinging to like a sinking ship.

When the world ends this time,
a group of boys play soccer in a gas station parking lot
while smoking cigarettes. They kick it into the street and

run into traffic and you wonder if they think of home. You
wonder if they write poetry in their heads, wonder if there's
anything your mind won't insist on turning into poetry.

When the world ends this time,
there will be no survivors to hear your confessions
this time around. You know this. But, look, some things
still need tending. The flowers in your vase are
wilting, so, look, there are still
things to do.

When the world ends this time,
you fly across the country into your friend's bed
and you don't hold her hand, but you kiss her good night.

You kiss her good night.

Acknowledgements

To Newark and the train from Penn Station to 33rd Street.

To the lights on the Chattanooga bridge, best viewed past midnight by the shore.

To my aunt's pousada by the beach in Florianópolis and the four pairs of Havaianas in my closet.

To the mountains and abandoned trailers I escaped to in Tranquility (I'm not sorry for the search parties).

To Riverside for its coffee, its passion, its want for more that propelled my own desires.

To Recreational Coffee and No Pulp Poetry in Long Beach, the communities that embraced me when I most needed it.

To California for being the birthplace of Pluto's and some of my best work.

To cappuccinos in mugs and iced flat whites (with whole milk).

To everyone I've had writing sessions with.

To my notes app that has seen one too many late-night thoughts.

To the love and hate that drove me to write these poems.

To those I love and hate.

To everyone I've left behind and held onto:
I don't regret a thing.

Actual Acknowledgements

Thank you to all of the places I've called home, even the ones I struggled to love: Vancouver, Canada; Carazinho, Brasil; Tranquility, New Jersey; Newark, New Jersey; Hamburg, Pennsylvania; Baltimore, Maryland; Chattanooga, Tennessee; Riverside, California; and Long Beach, California. Special thank you to Newark for being the place that raised me, the only place I can truly call my hometown. Thank you to the people who have made these places feel like home, too many to be named. Thank you to the beautiful and talented people who read and gave feedback on this work before anyone else—Miyin, George, Sofía, Lindsey. Thank you to Lori for your wonderful music and for working with me to release this poetry in different forms. Thank you, Kathleen, for your marketing expertise and advice. Thank you, Soleil and Stephanie, for designing my beautiful book cover. Thank you to my parents for dealing with the anxiety I've given them while living across the country. Thank you to the amazing band Dogs on Shady Lane for making the song Cole St and allowing me to use it in my epigraph. And as always, thank you to everyone reading this, everyone who has supported my work, whether through my writing or through Pluto's. When the world ends, I know where I'll run to—I hope you do, too.

About the Author

Paula Macena is, above all, a writer. Besides this, she's a Brazilian-American who (mostly) grew up in New Jersey and currently resides in California. In her pursuit of providing a platform for writers, she is the founder and director of Pluto's, an organization that makes literature accessible to all. When she's not reading or writing, you can find her making coffee.